My Neighborhood
The Park

Megan Cuthbert

AV² provides enriched content that supplements and complements this book. Weigl's AV² books strive to create inspired learning and engage young minds in a total learning experience.

Your AV² Media Enhanced books come alive with...

Audio
Listen to sections of the book read aloud.

Key Words
Study vocabulary, and complete a matching word activity.

Video
Watch informative video clips.

Quizzes
Test your knowledge.

Go to **www.av2books.com**, and enter this book's unique code.

BOOK CODE

Q267817

Embedded Weblinks
Gain additional information for research.

Slide Show
View images and captions, and prepare a presentation.

AV² by Weigl brings you media enhanced books that support active learning.

Try This!
Complete activities and hands-on experiments.

... and much, much more!

Published by AV² by Weigl
350 5th Avenue, 59th Floor New York, NY 10118
Websites: www.av2books.com   www.weigl.com

Library of Congress Control Number: 2014940864

ISBN 978-1-4896-1318-9 (hardcover)
ISBN 978-1-4896-1319-6 (softcover)
ISBN 978-1-4896-1320-2 (single user eBook)
ISBN 978-1-4896-1321-9 (multi-user eBook)

Printed in the United States of America in North Mankato, Minnesota
1 2 3 4 5 6 7 8 9 0 18 17 16 15 14

052014
WEP150314

Project Coordinators: Heather Kissock and Katherine Balcom
Design: Mandy Christiansen

Every reasonable effort has been made to trace ownership and to obtain permission to reprint copyright material. The publishers would be pleased to have any errors or omissions brought to their attention so that they may be corrected in subsequent printings.

Weigl acknowledges Getty Images as the primary image supplier for this title.

The Park

CONTENTS

This is my neighborhood.

The park is in my neighborhood.

The park is a green space in my neighborhood.

The park makes my neighborhood a nice place to visit.

I learn about nature when I go to the park.

There are many different animals and plants to see.

My park is a fun place for me to play with my friends.

We can run and play outdoor games together.

Sometimes my art class goes to the park to paint.

We practice painting the things we see.

My park has a day camp where I can go on the weekend.

I can make new friends and learn new crafts.

People use the park to hold special events.

We go to see plays and music festivals in the park.

My family has picnics in the park.

I love to go to the park.

Sometimes people in my neighborhood work together to clean the park.

We all need to pick up the cans and paper that litter the green space.

See what you have learned about parks.

Which of these pictures does not show a park?

KEY WORDS

Research has shown that as much as 65 percent of all written material published in English is made up of 300 words. These 300 words cannot be taught using pictures or learned by sounding them out. They must be recognized by sight. This book contains 47 common sight words to help young readers improve their reading fluency and comprehension. This book also teaches young readers several important content words, such as proper nouns. These words are paired with pictures to aid in learning and improve understanding.

Page	Sight Words First Appearance
4	is, my, this
5	in, the
6	a
7	makes, place, to
8	about, go, I, learn, when
9	and, animals, are, different, many, plants, see, there
10	for, me, play, with
11	can, run, together, we
12	sometimes
13	things
14	day, has, on, where
15	new
16	people, use
18	family
20	together, work
21	all, need, paper, that, up

Page	Content Words First Appearance
4	neighborhood
5	park
6	green space
8	nature
10	friends
11	games
12	art class, paint
14	camp, weekend
15	crafts
16	events
17	music festivals, plays
18	picnics

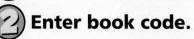